What people are saying about

Class And The Evangelical Chu...
introduction to the problems that the predominanty middle-class evangelical constituency face when looking to reach
the whole nation for Christ. Using both scholarly techniques
and statistics, alongside pithy and powerful quotes straight
from the horse's mouth, Birkett lays a foundation which every
church leader needs to be aware of, in order for them to begin
to consider how to reach those parts of the community which
are often, if not forgotten, usually long left behind by much of
the Church and can feel too alien to engage.

Jonathan Macy, Church of The Cross, Thamesmead;
joint author of the Church of England Evangelical Council's
'Privilege, Class & Poverty'.

This is an insightful and important short book addressing the
issue of class and the Christian church in the UK. The British are renowned for being bound by 'class' and the Christian
community has not escaped being shaped by sub-Christian
preferences. The fact that 0.9 percent of people in the most
deprived parishes attend church, compared with 2.4 per cent
in the least deprived (one of the fascinating statistics in the
Appendix) must surely give us pause for thought and prayer.
Those of us in 'middle class' churches should read, mark and
inwardly digest the message of this book.

Mike Neville, St Simon Zealots Church, London.

I wish I had read this book before I started ministry. It would have helped me so much. Nevertheless, I am grateful for it now, not least for Kirsten Birkett's gospel-hearted approach and insightful perspective. I am so encouraged by the way this book connects with working class people and their need for the gospel. I spent thirteen years as Vicar in a parish that was mainly working class, and, in that way, was similar to the area I grew up in. Yet my formative experiences in evangelical Christianity, my ministry training and the networks in which I mix have been dominated by people from a 'posh' background. This book helps understand and appreciate both, and for me, disentangles some of the confusion I have been struggling with for years.

George Crowder, Cheadle Parish Church, Chester.

60% of people in Britain consider themselves working class. Kirsten Birkett contends that while Christianity rightly priorities evangelism, middle-class churches in England, at present, will not reach the working classes, for Christian morality is too often unconsciously conflated with middle-classness. Why do we instinctively do the things we do? How do we see those different to us? How are we heard by those different to us? How may the gospel transform how we actually do church? Riding upon a wave of striking statistics, thorough research, probing questions, and compelling testimonies, Birkett sounds a clarion call for all middle-class churches to examine their unconscious social and cultural bias, all so that the good news of Jesus Christ may reach the least, the last, and the lost. A must-read for all middle-class Christians.

Sam Ashton, St Paul's Anglican Church, Hadley Wood.

Kirsten hits the nail on the head when it comes to ministering to the working class. As a lad from a council estate in the North West of England, this book has been music to my ears. It challenges us on how we live with, minister to and train people from working-class backgrounds. The challenge to cross-culture mission from middle-class evangelical churches to reach the working class is to be admired and acted upon. May God use this book to challenge our thinking and bring more people to Him through what has been written.

Mark Wilson, St James and St Paul's, West Bromwich

Class and the Evangelical Church in England

Kirsten Birkett

Class and the Evangelical Church in England
by Kirsten Birkett
© Church Society 2024

Church Society
Ground Floor, Centre Block
Hille Business Estate,
132 St Albans Road
Watford WD24 4AE, UK
Tel +44 (0)1923 255410
www.churchsociety.org
admin@churchsociety.org

Printed in the UK
ISBN: 978-1-7395160-7-9

Table of contents

Chapter 1

Introduction

'I wanted to be a pastor. But it didn't seem to be something that a working-class man could do.' (Retired working-class Anglican man.)

'I felt like an NCO walking into the Officer's Mess.' (Working-class pastor on his experience of attending an evangelical conference.)

'My first thought was: they're going to cover up this one, too.' (Working-class evangelical Christian on hearing of accusations against a prominent upper-class clergyman.)

'My great-grandfather had to doff his hat at the squire. Didn't matter how good a man he was or how bad a man the squire was. It made my grandfather full of fury. I still get angry about it when I hear posh accents.'

In 2020, still in the throes of lockdown, I was asked to think about and write some observations on class in the evangelical church in England. Those who asked me apparently thought that my Australian background gives me an advantage; I am not embedded in the British class system myself, so can be more objective. I'm not sure that this was all that much an advantage: class in Britain is a very complicated and deeply-entrenched matter, not at all easy to understand. It still surprises me that even after eighteen years living and working in Britain, I find certain aspects of the class system entirely foreign. Reading and researching on class issues has demonstrated that there is a lot that even now I had never realised, in particular how powerful are the emotions and attitudes involved. The classes are different, in significant ways, and it really matters to people.

There are class structures in Australian society, but they work differently. The label 'class' is much less historically embedded, and was never as stratified. There was never an actual aristocracy. From the start there were people who were wealthier and better educated, and through the nineteenth century as the country opened up there was a difference between those who owned property and/or were employers, and those who worked for them. Today there certainly exists a divide between the university-educated and those who are not.

My own family exemplifies a move between these strata. Both my parents grew up in relatively deprived circumstances, and both of them were the first of their families ever to have tertiary education (they both trained as teachers). They made considerable sacrifices to ensure that their children were well-educated and went to university; most of my cousins, on the other hand, entered trades or non-professional employment (not all of them). So I can sympathise, to some extent, with working-class culture. But I am writing this from a far more middle-class personal position, in both Australia and the UK. My conclusions come from research, not from personal experience.

Those conclusions are that running middle-class churches will not reach the working classes. This strategy will not be evangelistically successful, any more than running English-speaking churches in China would. There are exceptions and miracles, and small successes; they do not change the basic issues.

What I have also discovered is that what I will be saying is nothing new.[1] Plenty of research has been done, and good books written, on class in the evangelical church, from the academic level to the general. The statistics and the analyses are out there. Books and papers provide summaries of

1 It is also something recognised internationally; for instance, it was the reason for founding Vocational Bible College, Sydney, www.vbc.edu.au.

government and academic research, collections of personal testimony, insightful analysis and practical suggestions.[2] Working-class Christian authors testify to years of being ignored or overlooked by otherwise faithful evangelicals who don't believe that there is a problem, or fail to do anything about it. Yet some of the voices they record tell a poignant story. 'The people didn't dress like me, they didn't talk like me, they didn't socialize like me … Even the humour they used was different; nothing was the same.'[3]

Evangelical churches are not reaching the working class. It is not that they necessarily lack conscious ministry to the poor; a lot of churches have social action projects, and even see people come to faith. 'But often,' Williams and Brown comment, 'we then struggle to help them find true belonging and community in the church.'[4]

2 Two particularly helpful books, both well-researched and accessible, are: Natalie Williams and Paul Brown, *Invisible Divides: Class, Culture and Barriers to Belonging in the Church* (London: SPCK, 2022) and Mez McConnell, *The Least, the Last and the Lost: Understanding Poverty in the UK and the Responsibility of the Local Church* (Leyland, Evangelical Press; 2021).

3 Williams and Brown, *Invisible Divides*, 9. Of course, class is not the only division that creates this kind of experience. It could be applied to race, or foreignness in general, or age, marital status or sexuality, and will differ from church to church. There are many groups that can potentially find themselves in a minority and feeling excluded in church, and that should never happen for anyone. Here, however, we are focussing particularly on class.

4 Williams and Brown, *Invisible Divides*, 7.

More commonly, the gospel is not being preached and churches are not being established amongst working-class communities. Writers report instead a sense of disdain for the working class, the 'chavs' who claim benefits, hang around on street corners, work as trainee hairdressers, cleaners, bar staff and security guards, eat Pot Noodles and McDonalds and drink cheap cider. As Williams and Brown say, 'the danger in any church where there is a majority culture is that we assume that that culture's habits and traditions and ways of doing things are "right" and others are "wrong"'.[5]

It is not just evangelicals who appear to be blind to the effects of class in British religion. Some scholars have noticed this absence in understanding religion in general:

> The virtual absence of social class in the sociology of religion is almost as mysterious as it is telling. Long one of the central organising concepts in the discipline as a whole (particularly in the UK), there has been a dearth of discussion about class in the sociology of religion, just as class analysis has been markedly inattentive to the role of religion in the formation of classes and class subjectivities.[6]

Nor is this a purely modern problem, as Peter Ackers ob-

---

5 Williams and Brown, *Invisible Divides*, 12.

6 Andrew McKinnon, 'Religion and Social Class: Theory and Method After Bourdieu', *Sociological Research Online* 22.1 (2017): 161–173, 15.

serves:

> The British educated classes have long worried and fantasized about working-class religious belief and unbelief. Anglican churchmen feared Methodist "enthusiasm" in the eighteenth century, radicalism in the aftermath of the French Revolution, and urban, industrial irreligion after the 1851 Religious Census on churchgoing.[7]

Traditionally the English educated classes feared there was too much working-class religion, not too little; but they still did not understand working-class religion, and did not feel it reflected 'real' Christianity. The problem of misunderstanding, and underlying judgement, remains; and with the decline of working-class gospel churches, this means large parts of British population remain unevangelized.

Yet evangelical Christians want to reach the nation. Conservative evangelicals have discussed and researched evangelism and church planting in considerable depth over the past few decades, and that research involves, as Joanne McKenzie says, 'considerable discussion of strategies for more effective ministry outside of the middle classes'.[8] Mid-

7   Peter Ackers, 'Protestant Sectarianism in Twentieth-Century British Labour History: From Free and Labour Churches to Pentecostalism and the Churches of Christ', *International Review of Social History*, 64 (2019): 129–142, 129.

8 Joanne McKenzie, 'A Different Class? Anglican Evangelical Leaders' Perspectives on Social Class', in Abby Day (ed.), *Contemporary Issues in the Worldwide Anglican Communion: Powers and*

dle-class evangelicals want people to be saved, and want people to be helped; they want to be generous and welcoming. What, then, is going wrong?

There seem to be a number of issues that are easily confused when discussing class and the church. Some of these issues overlap, but all need addressing.

What is the working class?

I find that in casual conversation the term 'working class' is tossed around as if everyone knows what it means. Yet secular as well as Christian writers struggle to define what the 'working class' is and who belongs to it. Even when considerable time is spent on careful definition and description of categories, it is easy for the discussion to slide from one definition to another. Do we mean people who live on council estates? People who work in manual labour? People without university degrees? Those on benefits? If you have none of these things, does that make you middle class – or is it possible to be a working class person with a degree and a professional job? Many writers say that it is – that in fact working classness has more to do with attitudes and feelings than (necessarily) economic or geographical location.

Should people stop being working class?

Is that what the aim is – to move everyone out of poverty/

Pieties (Farnham: Ashgate, 2016), 170–189, 170–71.

benefits dependency/menial work/working class culture to property ownership/ 'meaningful' work/middle-class values? Is it right to aim for all of Britain to become middle class, as various politicians over the years have suggested? Is there not *anything* good about being working class that society, and churches, might want to preserve and champion? Asking this question brings us to:

What exactly is a Christian culture?

What sort of lives do we want people to have? If by social action we somehow managed to get everyone out of poverty, how ought they to live? What would socialising look like? Hospitality? Sharing? Homes? Dress? How much time would we spend together and what would we do?

What exactly is the problem with the middle-class church culture?

Is it that it is too 'intellectual', with long, difficult sermons? Is it too book-based? Is it a manner of speaking that tends to the indirect and values politeness over honesty? Is it an assumption that money should be accumulated and invested? Is it an insular nuclear family that puts children's education on a pedestal? Is it a failure to preach and practice self-sacrifice?

Do we want everyone, really, to be middle class? The failure of evangelical churches to reach the working classes has many dimensions, and part of it is a failure to challenge all cultures with the Bible.

There are some non-negotiables. For instance, Christianity is word-based. It requires a book. Christians have always spread literacy and education for precisely this reason. This need not be a problem for any class, and it should not ever be assumed that 'working class' means 'less intellectually able'. The Bible itself assumes that people are capable of hearing and understanding Scripture. Any church service must include the word taught and responded to in some way. Moreover, there are a whole host of moral behaviours that are required by Scripture, including honesty in speech and work, hospitality, faithfulness in marriage, purity of conduct and responsible management of families. What exactly it looks like to live according to these values, however, can encompass a wide range of social types; and it may be that aspects of working-class culture embody them better than middle-class culture.

This seems to be where the majority of commentators see the problem with the evangelical church in Britain. 'Middle-class values have become confused with biblical values', suggest Williams and Brown.[9] For that reason, those who

9 Williams and Brown, *Invisible Divides*, 12.

have not grown up with middle-class values feel either that they are forced to change unnecessarily in order to conform to church culture, or that they are excluded altogether by that culture. Moreover, when new churches are planted, they fail to preach to anyone who does not already have similar values. This means not only that whole sections of society are not reached with the gospel, but that middle-class Christians are not being rightly challenged to conform to Christ.

There is definitely a problem. Even though other problems in the church might seem to be looming larger at the moment, this problem – that whole swathes of the country never hear the gospel – is actually more important.

This book is addressed to my fellow middle-class evangelical Christians and their middle-class evangelical churches, to encourage them to do something about this situation. As I said at the beginning, the research has been done. It is out there. We need to start listening.

Where this book is going

This short book can only give a general overview of issues to do with class and the church. In chapter 2 we will consider just what we mean by class, and how working class is to be defined; then in chapter 3 we consider to what extent the evangelical church has taken on middle-class values. We consider these attitudes and values of the middle class in chapter 4, and how what is taught in evangelical churches has frequently reflected class more than biblical truth.

When we talk about 'class and the church', the emphasis is usually on the working class(es). It is not often about the upper class, increasingly a smaller proportion of British society. Yet there are those on that end of the social scale who may equally feel out of place and unwelcomed in the average middle-class evangelical church; perhaps not so much in London or university cities, but in other places around the country. The upper classes are as difficult to define as any other class in modern Britain, but we take a brief look at this issue in chapter 5.

In chapter 6 we return to the middle class, and consider whether middle-class values are all bad, and what might need to change. Chapter 7 is about theological education, which is overwhelmingly undertaken in a university setting or with university validation, and how that might need to change, or not, given class issues.

Chapter 8 looks at the role of mercy ministries, and whether churches should be undertaking more social action in their efforts to evangelise the working class. Finally in chapter 9 we think about practical action, and what the evangelical church might need to do if proper evangelisation of the country is to happen. An appendix and bibliography give some resources for further reading.

Chapter 2

Who are the working classes?

For centuries, medieval Britain was feudal. Aristocracy owned the land, and quite frequently the workers, too – or at least, the peasant (villein) workers – were tied to the land, and not free to leave it. On the other hand, this meant they were guaranteed a source of income. This system was remarkably stable for a long time, but this does not mean all workers were happy with it. Democracy was slow to spread; King John (1199–1216) was forced to reduce his authority with the famous document Magna Carta, but only in favour of his Barons. The parliamentary uprising under Oliver Cromwell in the English Civil War (1642–1651) gave more power to landowners as opposed to the nobility, but not to the common soldiers who fought for the victory.

Gradually feudalism gave way to a more modern system with an expanding middle class, and wealth began to move away from the land to trade and industry. The nineteenth century saw great changes as government began to rely more on elected representatives, and those without land agitated for universal suffrage. The nineteenth century also saw the rise of what we might consider the working class; a self-conscious group who worked for a living, on wages. These were the manual workers, the servants, the builders and labourers, the factory workers and miners and makers of things, as opposed to the landowners who accepted their rents and paid their wages.

World wars, the welfare state, the 'right to buy' council property and other social changes mean that the picture is different now, although British society is still very stratified. While the term 'working class' is still very much in use, it is a term that covers various different groups, and it is not the only way of understanding how society is divided.

Somewhere vs anywhere

For instance, a few years ago journalist David Goodhart introduced the idea of 'somewhere people' as opposed to 'anywhere people'. These terms cover some of the distinctions we are trying to understand.[1]

'Somewhere people' are that 50 percent or so of the population who think of themselves as attached to a certain place and a certain group within that place. They belong somewhere, whether that is Liverpool, the Scottish High-

1 David Goodhart, *The Road to Somewhere: The New Tribes Shaping British Politics* (London: Penguin, 2017).

lands, or within earshot of the Bow Bells. They feel strong connections with their communities and the communities' histories. Family ties with the place may go back generations.

Goodhart calls this an ascribed identity; an identity given by the place and by their community. Family, security and community are generally very important to them, and are the basis of their loyalties, tastes, activities and political preferences. They are less likely to have a university degree and are more likely to settle in the same place as they grew up.

'Anywhere people', on the other hand, think of themselves not in terms of their place but in terms of their work and achievements. Their identity is achieved; they think of themselves in terms of life experience. They are the people who expect to be able to fit in anywhere, and they often do travel and move in order to gain new experience. They value freedom, diversity and fluidity.

They are more likely to be university graduates, and the experience of university is part of creating the sense of anywhere. Their identity becomes more tied to their life development than their place of birth, and may be suspicious of group attachments. Goodhart sees this group as about 25 percent of the UK.

While the two groups might be characterised by certain types of education, income and work, the real difference is how they see themselves in relation to the wider world.

Somewhere people belong somewhere. Anywhere people can go anywhere. For Goodhart, this went some way to explaining the surprising result of the Brexit vote. The large group of Somewheres did not generally value the relationship with Europe nor the freedom to move between countries.

You do not need to meet with many communities across the UK to feel the resonance of this analysis. While Goodhart could be criticised in various details, there is a strong general truth to his description, and it ties very much into understanding modern class distinctions.

McConnell, for instance, writes of choice as a distinction between working and middle class. 'People from more affluent backgrounds can decide where they want to live, what job they'd like to take, and what school their children can be educated in. In short, *they have choices*. People who live in council estates have fewer choices, and often none.'[2]

The lower you are on the class scale, too, the less chance you have of upward mobility; of improving your employment or education, and so having more choices of where to live, holiday and socialise. Also you may well likely have a family background or local culture that does not encourage or directly opposes working hard in school and achieving, regardless of the quality of the teaching or innate intelligence.

---

2 Mez McConnell, *The Least, the Last and the Lost*, 101, his emphasis.

Different kinds of capital

It was probably the philosopher John Dewey (1859–1952) who first used the term 'social capital', referring to the networks of relationships that help society run and which give individuals advantages in life. It functions as an asset, just as financial capital (having more money) does. How well you do in life, then, is not just a matter of your wealth in economic terms. There are other kinds of capital, and sometimes a wealth of social capital can help people more – and be more valued – than mere financial capital. Another kind of capital is cultural capital, referring to the kind of culture you can access and enjoy: opera, fine art and restaurants or movies, TV and football. When you are able to speak about and take part in 'higher' culture, you have access to a different group of people, and so gain a particular kind of social capital, that is not available to someone who can't afford (and doesn't like) such things.

In Britain, London and the southeast of England holds the people with the most social, economic and cultural capital. That is where they are concentrated and where they gravitate; it is where the jobs are with the highest of each kind of capital, and you can probably only afford to move there if you can access a variety of capitals. The North has traditionally, and still has, fewer such people and less access to those capitals.

Working class lack of economic capital used to be allayed to some extent by their social capital – friends and family who could put a good word in with the mine foreman or the factory boss. But the loss of primary industries and the forced dislocation of communities has broken down such capital to a large extent.

Class distinctions, then, cannot be understood simply in terms of wealth or of earning power. It is also about what your money gives you access to. Even with money, if a person does not feel comfortable in a social group, he or she will not be able to access that social capital. Different kinds of social and cultural capital also teach different attitudes to money; what to do with it, how to value it, how to handle it.

Type of job

Sociologically, there are different groups that are lumped together in 'working class'. A generation or so ago, working class people were those whose dads worked down the mine or at the factory. For many, there was a certain work ethic and community spirit that went along with that; a pride in being able to pay the bills, never accepting charity and valuing family; probably a strong commitment to the union and the Labour Party.

However various different social changes undermined this type of working class. One was simply the decline of UK industry, hastened by the Thatcher government policies that opposed the unions.

Since 1994, the Office for National Statistics has analysed social strata based on occupation without using the word 'class' at all.[3] It has eight categories, with 'higher managerial, administrative and professional occupations' at the top and 'never worked and long-term unemployed' at the bottom. However five out of the eight categories describe jobs that in other contexts would easily be called 'working class'. Category 3 is 'intermediate occupations' (clerical, sales and service, technical services); four covers employers in small organisations in industry, commerce, services and agriculture, or 'own-account' workers in these areas; five is lower supervisory or technical occupations, six semi-routine occupations, and seven routine occupations ('routine' referring to the nature of the work – repetitive, under supervision).[4] In other words, there are a wide range of different jobs that could be considered working class.

3 Office for National Statistics, 'National Statistics Socio-economic Classification (NS-SEC)' https://www.ons.gov.uk/methodology/classificationsandstandards/otherclassifications/thenationalstatisticssocioeconomicclassificationnssecrebasedonsoc2010. See also Mike Savage et al, 'A New Model of Social Class? Findings from the BBC's Great British Class Survey Experiment', *Sociology* 47.2 (2013) 219–250.

4 'These positions have the least need for employee discretion and employees are regulated by a basic labour contract.' Office for National Statistics, 'NS-SEC'.

How you vote

It is commonplace to assume that working-class people vote Labour. Research suggests, however, that we should not conflate the two groups, now or at any other time in British history. By 1910 there was a 'working-class movement', largely affiliated with the Labour party, which had a cohesive effect for the working classes. But, as Ackers points out, 'For the rest of the century, British trade unions remained sectional interest groups, divided by skill, status, and industry'.[5] They represented the 'organized working classes' but in 1940 this was still only 33.1 percent; and Labour, at its best in the interwar years, had no more than half the working-class vote. Many manual workers 'never joined a union or voted Labour, still less shopped mainly at the Co-operative store. Both religion and political activism were strongest in the "respectable" working class'.[6]

Where you live

Most people who live in council estates, schemes or equivalent, would probably be included in and consider themselves working-class. These are the people highlighted by Mez McConnell. Even then, this category covers very different people. There will be traditional and skilled working class peo-

---

5 Ackers, 'Protestant Sectarianism', 131.
6 Ackers, 'Protestant Sectarianism', 132.

ple there, in trades or service jobs. There are also unskilled workers, shop assistants or waiters, factory workers, warehouse operatives, delivery drivers, cleaners, labourers for the trades. There are self-employed entrepreneurs; mobile hairdressers, gardeners, window-washers. Also, the long-term unemployed on benefits. The drug dealers. Sex workers. Immigrants and asylum seekers.

'There are many decent, hard-working, family-conscious people who live here', says McConnell. 'There are also many who are not so decent, not so hard working and not so family conscious. There is little doubt that there is a hardcore of those we can only describe as an underclass.'[7] Some love it, and some want to get out – or at least get their children out.

Habitus

The French sociologist Pierre Bordieu introduced the idea of 'habitus' in understanding social groupings,[8] and it has been taken up widely in understanding class. Habitus goes beyond external markers of any particular groups, and describes rather the internalised assumptions, thoughts and ways of being and acting that any group takes on. The differences between middle class and working class, then, can involve a whole range of things that go to make up a person: 'accent,

7 McConnell, *The Least, the Last and the Lost*, 157.
8 See Pierre Bordieu, *Outline of a Theory of Practice* (Cambridge: Cambridge University Press, 1977).

holidays, sports, media consumption, dress, food, the extent to which people live in the moment or plan for the future, whether they have chaotic or orderly lives and understandings of the family and parenting'.[9]

'Habitus' can also help us to understand differences within what are called classes. For instance, 'middle class' can cover different types of habitus. A public-school-educated city banker may be considered middle-class, but could be a world away from the primary school teacher in a northern city – in money, education, job prospects, networks, holidays, types of socialising, and ideas about social norms. 'Middle class' is not really a useful category in this sense; but we can gain a sense of the 'habitus' of different people.

The working-class habitus, however, is distinctive, and is hard to overcome, involving an indwelling feeling of being judged poorly. It seems to be a constant sense of self-doubt, very different from the internal confidence often instilled by middle-class schooling. 'The working class are never free from the judgements of imaginary and real others that position them, not just as different, but as inferior, as inadequate', one researcher puts it. This means that working class people 'can never have the certainty that they are doing it right which

---

9 McKenzie, 'A Different Class?', 175; also '"The Person God Made Me to Be": Navigating Working-Class and Christian Identities in English Evangelical Christianity', *Sociological Research Online*, 22.1, 11.

is one of the main signifiers of middle-class dispositions.'[10]

This brings us to one of the most powerful markers of being working class: how you feel.

How you feel

In recent literature, the aspect of what it feels like to be working class is coming more and more to the fore. What makes a working class person is not their job, their wealth or lack of it, or where they come from; it is very much how they feel.

'Probably the biggest, most disregarded and possibly most surprising and overlooked measure of class is, as with poverty, related to *feelings*',[11] writes Mez McConnell. 'Your class isn't about where you live. It's an attitude or a belief. It is more about where your head is than where your home is.'[12] And a lot of it is a feeling of despair: 'The feeling that no matter how hard you work, nothing ever changes.'[13]

One of the qualities that creates resilience in life is self-efficacy; a belief that you can accomplish what you set out to do. It's very hard to develop such self-belief in deprived circumstances, where nothing you do changes anything, and

---

10 B. Skeggs, *Formations of Class and Gender: Becoming Respectable* (London: Sage, 1997), 90, quoted in McKenzie, '"The Person God Made Me to Be"', 7.

11 McConnell, *The Least, the Last and the Lost*, 111, his emphasis.

12 Quoted in McConnell, *The Least, the Last and the Lost,* 117.

13 McConnell, *The Least, the Last and the Lost*, 125.

everyone tells you that anything you do won't make a difference. This is part of why deprivation remains persistent. Similarly, depression which can be caused by deprivation in turn robs people of the ability to try to overcome it.

Yet we must not conflate 'working class' with 'non-working class'. The working class still exists, and a lot of them are working. They build our houses and unblock our drains. They deliver our Amazon parcels. They collect the bins. They drive trains and buses. They work in care homes. They kept everything going during lockdown because they couldn't afford to stay at home (and so were more likely to catch covid).[14] They even voted for the Tories in 2019.

They are all being served poorly by the evangelical church. 'When would any of them have an opportunity to hear the gospel proclaimed?' asks McConnell of the hairdressers, electricians and other working friends who attended his father's birthday party. Many of them won't.

'There is quite clearly a fault line in the UK evangelical world. All men and women are not equal when it comes to having access to the gospel and discipleship-oriented resources.'[15] And because working class-ness is about feelings,

---

14 Social Mobility Barometer - public attitudes to social mobility in the UK (11 March 2021) https://www.gov.uk/government/publications/social-mobility-barometer-2021/social-mobility-barometer-public-attitudes-to-social-mobility-in-the-uk.

15 McConnell, *The Least, the Last and the Lost*, 28.

not just money or job, there are a lot of British people who feel working class even though they have university degrees and own property. They may technically fit into the middle class, but they don't feel welcomed by middle-class churches or the people in them. Whether it's the unemployed, frustrated and freezing person, a single mum on benefits, the tradesman with a thriving business, or the office worker with a degree who grew up on the estate, up to 60 percent of people in Britain are not hearing the gospel because they are excluded by our churches.

That's a problem.

Chapter 3

Class in the evangelical church

Evangelicals in Britain are overwhelmingly white and middle class. 93 percent of evangelicals in England label themselves 'White British' (compared to 81.7 percent in England and Wales). They have a high average age with 58 percent having been born before 1960, 32 percent in the 1960s or 1970s and only 10 percent since 1980. They belong to a wide range of Christian denominations, but at least a third are Church of England. 73 percent are higher professionals or intermediate professionals. 41 percent of English evangelicals have postgraduate qualifications. In the May 2015 general election 31 percent of English evangelicals voted Conservative, 25 percent Labour, 17 percent Liberal Democrat, 11.5 percent UKIP and 8 percent Green.[1]

It is good when any people come to know the living God and worship him in church. The problem, however,

1 Greg Smith and Linda Woodhead 'Religion and Brexit: populism and the Church of England', *Religion, State and Society* 46.3 (2018): 206–223.

when any group is dominant in any setting is that it assumes that its own way of doing things is normal. The way things are done becomes not just the right way, but the only way. It is very easy in such contexts to be oblivious to the way in which the majority way excludes people who come from a different group.

Evangelicals are aware of their class profile, and in many cases actively fight against it. They realise that evangelical ministry must disrupt class boundaries. As McKenzie acknowledges, they know that the gospel means 'the equality, dignity and value of all people, regardless of social status, in the family of God and to speak of a spiritual reality that should be reflected in the corporate life of the church and the local congregation'.[2] Moreover, many will teach that:

> ... social reconciliation between human beings was seen to be a necessary outworking of the reconciliation with God achieved through Christ's death. The grace and inclusion that God extends to people through Christ was understood to necessitate demonstrable grace and the inclusion of all people within the church community, including those of different social classes, in order to reflect the nature of the gospel to the world.[3]

People in evangelical ministry also acknowledge their middle-class way of doing ministry, McKenzie says.

2 McKenzie, 'A Different Class?', 176.
3 McKenzie, 'A Different Class?', 176.

> Certain forms of Bible teaching, an emotion-
> ally restrained mode of communication, styles
> of music used in worship, rationalist apologetic
> methods and the corporate business-like mood
> of many evangelical services were identified
> as potentially intimidating or alien to work-
> ing-class culture and were felt to contribute to
> a 'self-perpetuating system' of disengagement.[4]

Yet despite understanding all this, and despite their determination for class not to be an issue, evangelicals seem to have
been singularly ineffective in eliminating the boundaries.

Leadership in the evangelical church

There are some working-class people in ministry leadership
within British evangelical churches. On the whole, however, they can feel very isolated, as any minority does: 'you
go to Christian conferences and the male speakers are different kinds of men to working-class men', one interviewee
comments.[5] The style of middle-class leadership, moreover,
tends to be very different from working class culture: distinctive in dress and grooming, with a certain kind of humour
and (as mentioned above) emotionally restrained. Working
class culture, on the other hand, is 'more open, upfront and
passionate'. Preaching and teaching the Bible and evangelism
– practices central to evangelical ministry – all seem to be

4 McKenzie, 'A Different Class?', 178.

5 Joanne McKenzie, 'The Person God Made Me to Be', 5.

done in a distinctly middle-class way. This is reflected in interviews:

> Noah expressed his feeling that there is 'a glass ceiling with regard to leadership' within evangelicalism in relation to class; working-class leaders can feel a lack of legitimation despite their shared commitment to the theological and doctrinal positions that are valued within the movement. [6]

The result is that middle class ways of doing ministry 'are more easily accepted as the "right" way to do things'.[7]

Working-class people, then, even when gifted, properly trained and committed to ministry, can feel considerable doubts about being 'the wrong sort of person' for Christian ministry.[8] 'People like us don't do it' appears to be a common feeling – evangelical ministry is 'not for the likes of us'. Even those who are quite certain and confident that they possess

---

6 McKenzie, 'The Person God Made Me to Be', 6.

7 McKenzie, 'The Person God Made Me to Be', 6.

8 As seen in the report '"Let Justice Roll Down Like Waters": Exploring the Wellbeing of Working-Class Clergy in the Church of England: A Rally Cry for Change' (October 2023), https://www. churchofengland.org/sites/default/files/2023-10/focussed-study-4-working-class-clergy-wellbeing.pdf. The C of E has recently made the selection criteria for ordination less exclusive to attract more working-class ordinands; see Madeleine Davies, 'New selection framework seeks "unseen-called"', *Church Times* (25 June 2021), https://www.churchtimes.co.uk/articles/2021/25-june/news/uk/new-selection-framework-seeks-unseen-called.

the New Testament qualifications for leadership can still feel like frauds.

Working class in the pews

Churches can generate estrangement even where the ideals of equality and inclusivity exist. That can be precisely because middle-class people come into contact with other classes, and do not know what to do with the difference. For instance, the daily personal struggles that poorer people face, of living on a knife edge, and the worries and weariness of financial burdens, make life very different from those without financial burdens; these 'can produce feelings of isolation and distance from middle-class people who don't experience such struggle'.[9] I can remember the church worker who was asked by a couple in the congregation why he wasn't travelling home to visit his sick mother. They couldn't imagine what would be holding him back. He had to answer, in front of others, that he couldn't buy a ticket that day because there was no money in his account. That had simply not occurred to them. They had probably never in their adult lives had no money in their bank accounts.

When daily struggles and issues are very different, just how do you share honestly in a home group? Both the poor and the rich can be very uncomfortable with honest sharing; the poor feeling a sense of shame to confess poverty, the rich

9 McKenzie, 'A Different Class?', 182.

feeling a sense of burden or guilt that they are expected to cough up money to help (or not knowing if it's even appropriate to suggest it). Our society at large has deep inequalities, and these create 'hidden, embodied and psychosocial injuries.'[10] Working-class Christians can and do feel shame (and resentment) when the Christians around them seem to have so many more privileges than they do, and they feel judged for their lack.

Living on the edge financially is stressful. Worry, guilt and shame can be constant companions; this can lead to anger or resentment when people who have 'never struggled for anything in their lives ... are given the power to tell you how you should behave.' Middle class people can certainly face crises in their lives, but they are likely to be quite different sorts of crises. It is easy for a working class hearer to think that the middle class preacher has no idea of the realities of life faced. Moreover, such feelings of alienation are likely to be made worse by the 'emotional tempo and middle-class restraint embodied in the act of preaching.'[11] As one working-class person relates:

> If I go to a church and I'm a working-class man and I hear the middle-class preacher preach I'm probably not going to get any hint that he has struggle in his life, therefore, I'm going to say he

---

10 McKenzie, 'The Person God Made Me to Be', 2.

11 McKenzie, 'The Person God Made Me to Be', 7.

can't talk to me because he doesn't know what I've been through. And when he tells me about God's love and God's provision I'll be, like, 'It's alright for you, you've got your inheritance and you've got all like whatever, nice stuff in life: you can't talk to me'. When he talks to me about being forgiven and Christ's righteousness, I'll be like 'Well, that's all right for you, but you haven't done the bad things I've done'.[12]

Ministry resources for working class people

A common theme in working class comments about evangelicalism is the inappropriateness of most ministry resources. Evangelistic courses, discipleship courses and other ministry materials appear to be almost universally produced by and for middle-class people. Those in ministry to working-class audiences struggle to find materials they can use. The result is:

> ... you've got this self-perpetuating system. All the books that are written by British evangelicals are about middle-class Christianity and then that feeds even more into the system. And it means that when a working-class guy goes to get a book to help him in his Christian walk, he is forced to either acclimatize to middle-class culture and start becoming something that he isn't, or he says 'Forget this, this isn't for me'.

12 Quoted in McKenzie, 'The Person God Made Me to Be', 7.

Nothing tells me in these bookshops about how I deal with a baby mother who hates my guts and who won't let me see my kids and I've got to work out as a Christian what I do now. Am I free to marry someone else? Do I go through the court to get visitation rights? Or do I pray and fast and wait to see? What do I do? A young guy can't get a book on what do I do when I've just left a gang and there's the gang trying to get me back and I want to follow Jesus and another situation's come up and my family's threatened and the gang can help me and the church can't – what do I do?[13]

It is not as if British evangelicals deliberately try to exclude working-class people, or working-class ministry. On the contrary, as we have seen there is a great deal of interest in evangelising the working class. There seems, however, to be a massive blind spot when it comes to doing it. In practice, ministry style and resourcing is for middle-class people without a sense of how exclusive this is.

Making evangelicalism more available to working-class people is a clear priority of the gospel. Barriers should be being broken down, not reinforced. To do so, however, middle class evangelicals will need to become far more conscious of the way in which their culture embodies values that are not self-evident and are (at best) only one way to live Christianly.

13 Quoted in McKenzie, The Person God Made Me to Be', 7.

The gospel is far wider than is currently being practiced.

Chapter 4

Middle-class attitudes and values

Humans tend to have a whole range of views on what is the right and what is the wrong way to do things. As Christians, these views should be shaped by Scripture. Scripture, however, leaves us with a great deal of freedom to live life in different ways; we do not have a rule-book that covers everything, because the godly person is free to make personal decisions on a whole range of issues. Whether you prefer kale or broccoli, countryside or city streets, easy rock or hard-core classical, a great deal of how we live life day to day is a matter of Christian freedom.

Nonetheless, for most of us, our views easily solidify into something more judgemental than that. How we are brought up has a great deal to do with this; how the people in our church behave also affects us. It is very easy to conflate 'what our sort of people do' with 'what Christians should do'.

'We all learned how to behave, what to believe and how to talk as children. Money doesn't tend to change these norms, which is why class is not really about money'.[1] But class can involve set attitudes to a whole range of lifestyle issues, none of which are necessarily to do with Christian ethics – but Christians can nevertheless become very judgemental about them. Just a few areas in which such unconscious assumptions are treated as Christian ethics are listed below.

Smoking

In the UK around 13.3 percent of people aged 18 years and over smoke cigarettes. That is about around 6.6 million people. How would they feel in our churches? Would they feel completely comfortable about ducking outside during coffee time for a cigarette? I would guess, probably not. I would also guess that it would not be long before a well-meaning church member took that person aside to counsel them on giving up smoking. Such attitudes, however, would disproportionately affect working class people; in the UK, people with no qualifications are more likely to smoke (28.2 percent) than those with a degree (6.6 percent).

Money

Attitudes to money are frequently mentioned in the differences between middle-class and working-class people. It is not just a matter of how much money a person has or earns,

---

1 McConnell, *The Least, the Last and the Lost*, 136.

but what people do with it. Do we deride other people's ways of spending money? Why is ours any more Christian? Is it biblical to accumulate wealth? To have wealth to pass onto children?

Middle-class people are notoriously tight when it comes to giving money away. I am frequently astonished at the sacrificial generosity of people who have little to give, but still give it. A culture that instead values saving, investing and accumulating wealth, by definition hangs on to money. Moreover, that culture can become surprisingly judgemental towards those who do not hang onto their money so tightly; who do not save, who never aim to own property.

At the same time, I suspect middle class churches are relatively slow to condemn the sins of pride, gluttony, greed, and coveting, all of which are closely associated with attitudes to money. How much does your church challenge those who accumulate money rather than giving to the poor? What percentage of income are you encouraged to give away (and has anyone in your church actually mentioned a percentage?). After all, the more money you have, the greater percentage you can afford to part with – is that a challenge that has been made in your church?

Work

The middle-class attitude to work tends to revolve around achievement, status, personal satisfaction and a sense of meaning in life. Is work a means to an end, or something that gives you purpose? If your work is in a supermarket or answering phones at the council, there's little chance that you think of it in terms of purpose or fulfilment.

Middle-class preachers emphasise the dignity of work, and it is indeed a pre-fall creation ordinance. Yes, work is part of our purpose, but as Williams and Brown point out, 'in the western, middle-class world, for many this has been stretched to make specific work *the* purpose of our lives'.[2] Work is dignified because it allows us to eat; not because it gives us meaning, or purpose, or fulfilment. Personal fulfilment is to be found in the Great Commandments and the Great Commission. 'Where we work is not as important as the relationships we build'.[3]

Accents

> An Englishman's way of speaking absolutely classifies him.
>
> The moment he talks he makes some other Englishman despise him.[4]

British ears are very attuned to accents, especially when they relate to class differences. That wouldn't matter if there were

---

2 Williams and Brown, *Invisible Divides*, 105.

3 Williams and Brown, *Invisible Divides*, 107.

4 Alan Jay Lerner and Frederick Lowe, 'Why Can't the English', *My Fair Lady* (1956).

no judgements made on the basis of class; but when every class is prepared to judge another negatively, these indicators can be barriers. Such judgements are often made immediately, and unconsciously. It takes effort to be aware of one's own reactions, and to take conscious control of judgements. Whether your immediate reaction to another person's accent is positive or negative, we need to be aware of it so that we neither form cliques or subtly exclude anyone.

Middle-class reactions to regional or working-class accents can be devastating. One working-class academic relates her experience of being at an academic conference (where her qualifications, and research, absolutely entitled her to be). A dismissive comment was offered to her from the front, accompanied by general laughter: later, she read feedback sheets offering 'helpful advice' to her:

> Supposedly 'helpful' suggestions included that I enunciate 'properly', that I speak slower and breathe more because my accent was 'quite thick', scribbled alongside comments on my 'lack of confidence' and inability to 'project' my voice. I threw the comments away soon afterwards, on the advice of a friend, but over ten years later I still remember those comments and the way they made me feel.[5]

5 Sarah Marie Hall, '"You're not from 'round 'ere, are you?" Class, accent and dialect as opportunity and obstacle in research encounters', in *Engaging with Policy, Practice and Publics: Intersectionality and Impacts*, eds. Sarah Marie Hall and Ralistsa Hiteva

Probably some of the middle-class participants felt they were only joking, or being helpful, and would have been horrified at the hurt they caused. No doubt others were simply snobs and did not care. Either way, most appeared to be unconscious of their effect. Such unrecognised hurt could easily be occurring in evangelical churches.

Hospitality

Have you ever been invited around to someone's house for dinner? For most middle-class people, the answer is 'of course'. It's a very common way of socialising. There are a lot of people, however, who never socialise like that; people for whom sit-down dinner parties just never happen. Socialising instead happens at the pub, or another venue, and that is where people feel comfortable.

The rules around dinner parties are strict, but never explained, because it is assumed that everyone knows them. When you are invited to someone's house, there is generally an assumption (never stated, and denied if asked) that you

---

(Bristol and Chicago: Policy Press, 2020), 41–58, 53. Similar accent snobbishness is a barrier in other professions, too: see Natalie Braber et al., '"Is he a barrister or not?": A study on perceived and actual accentism at the Bar of England and Wales', The International Journal of Speech, Language and the Law (2024), https://doi.org/10.1558/ijsll.25886; also Erez Levon, Devyani Sharma and Christian Ilbury, 'Speaking up: accents and social mobility' (The Sutton Trust, November 2022).

should bring something. Chocolates, wine or flowers are acceptable; hot chocolate mix is not. A plant in a pot is acceptable; a cabbage is not. Without knowing the rules, however, a person is easily left baffled, ashamed and feeling thoroughly unwelcome.

The middle-class method of exercising hospitality by having people around for a meal can also be a way of failing to share life with them. How much do we go to people's houses just to be there? Not for a meal, but to spend the afternoon or evening? There is a totally different feel of sharing life when people know they do not need to wait for an invitation, but are welcome to come at any time, whatever is happening. The middle-class way of hospitality, however, tends to be strictly controlled. We want to put definite boundaries on when we are hospitable to others. That suits us; after all, middle-class people have busy lives. Visitors just dropping in might disrupt that.

What is served after church also easily embeds middle class assumptions about hospitality. I have heard the argument that having expensive coffee makes people feel welcome; but it can also make people feel excluded, if they never drink it anywhere else. Or it may be that only a certain kind of free-trade beverage is used, on the assumption that that is the best way to have a social conscience. The fact that this is a very middle-class attitude does not often come into the discussion.

Afterword: some things to reflect upon

1. Williams and Brown challenge us to think about the following assumptions:

> i. Home ownership is better than renting
>
> ii. Saving money is better than giving it away
>
> iii. The longer you stay in education the better
>
> iv. You should choose carefully the neighbourhood where you live
>
> v. You should try to send your children to the highest-achieving school
>
> vi. Being organized with a diary is a sign of spiritual maturity.[6]

Do you resonate with these assumptions? Or not? Why is that?

2. Picture yourself going to someone else's house for a meal. How many unspoken rules are there? Go through the evening and question everything you might do – how do you know what is expected?

3. Consider Ephesians 5:4 'Nor should there be obscenity, foolish talk or coarse joking, which are out of place'. What

---

6 Williams and Brown, *Invisible Divides*, 39.

does this actually mean? What is included and excluded? Why do you place the boundaries where you do?

4. Do we have church services or Bible study groups available for people on shift work? Have you ever been challenged to work less so you have more time for ministry? Has the idea of 'career' been challenged as being fundamentally self-centred?

5. How similar are the accents in your church? How do you feel when you hear someone with a regional or working-class accent? Do you assume that person is less well educated, less suitable to read the Bible out loud, less likely to be a good leader?

6. Are some jobs better than others? On what basis? Are there Bible verses that support your assumptions? Would you be happy for your child to be a hairdresser/ sandwich maker/ street sweeper? Why/why not?

7. What is your attitude to smoking (or vaping)? How would you react to having a smoker in your home group? Would you allow a fellow Christian to smoke inside your home?

Chapter 5

A brief note on the posh

Modern Britain developed out of a feudal system which had a ruling class of aristocracy. The landowning class was greatly expanded with the seizure of monastic lands under Henry VIII, and this class continued to dominate Britain for the next several centuries.

The two world wars of the early twentieth century were very hard on the upper class. Death duties cut into traditional wealth. Social attitudes were changing, and traditional privileges and respect given to the upper class waned in the new post-war Britain. The 1958 Life Peerages Act meant that entry to the House of Lords was no longer dominated by hereditary titles, instead opening entry to life peers of both sexes.

The traditional upper class – those who need not work, but live on inherited wealth on large inherited estates, perhaps with a title in the family – is now vanishingly small in Britain. However many have moved into what is now considered the upper middle class; sending their children to prestigious public schools, perhaps as boarders, and moving in circles that may include socialising with royalty and the peerage, with a distinct focus on country living and international holidays. They may no longer be called, or be, 'upper class' – rather the traditional upper class, and the upper-middle class, are perceived by the rest of the population as simply 'posh'.[1]

They are still very privileged, in economic, social and cultural capital. Their children grow up with a characteristic confidence and ability to take high paying jobs through a combination of social networks and the expectation of demanding – and receiving – good salaries. This confidence is no accident. Someone who begins boarding school aged seven needs to develop a certain independence and toughness. An atmosphere of competition with peers, and an instilled sense of being one of the elite (and needing to stay so), develops this toughness further. The independent school system is, indeed, institutionally designed to produce fierce independence. Such qualities are useful in the secular world, which values self-starting, hard-working, ambitious, resilient individuals. The same qualities are not always so useful for godliness. Of course shyness and lack of confidence can oc-

---

1 There is an interesting, and (I am told) not at all comfortable relationship between the traditionally upper-class and the nouveau riche, the newly wealthy who often aspire to be upper-class and can afford the property and the lifestyle.

cur in individuals in any class, but the dominant image of the products of posh upbringing and education is of confidence shading into arrogance and entitlement, an assumption that they are the best persons to be in charge in any situation and that leadership is therefore their duty and right.

Some of them become Christians, perhaps through the system of camps for independent school students begun by Revd Eric John Hewitson Nash ('Bash') in the 1930s, or other evangelistic efforts. Many such Christians have rejected a good many of their class assumptions, and often privileges. Some will go into ministry and live with considerable sacrifice, considering the potential wealth they could have earned elsewhere. Some will be very generous and finance valuable gospel initiatives (the founding of Cornhill training is a notable example). Posh people can provide invaluable service to the gospel, using their *entre* to powerful circles and social influence for Christ, and using their confidence and learned independence to stand up to ungodly influences in potentially very costly ways, and in ways that are just not available to those outside such circles.

Such confidence, however, can also blur into arrogance, even in Christian circles, even with the best of intentions. The assumption of leadership is not always warranted. Class boundaries can rub against each other, even amongst committed Christians who agree wholeheartedly on Christian principles. A certain supercilious attitude of superiority can be met by the angry chip on the shoulder. What makes the attitude of the posh even harder to bear for the lower classes is the seeming, or even actual, total unconsciousness with which it is held. 'How wonderful it is to be in Christ where there are no class differences', I remember an (I am sure genuinely) earnest young man praying in his highly cultured voice in a youth group I attended in Oxford. I looked surreptitiously around the circle of other young people, not all of whom were from the university, and encountered not a few incredulous glances and rolling of the eyes.

Those who are posh, whether strictly upper-class or upper-middle-class, will have grown up with considerable privilege that makes them much more likely to achieve in life. They may also work very hard and exercise considerable discipline – but they are in a position to do so, with the training to do so, which puts them at great advantage compared to those who grew up with no encouragement, skills or confidence. Those without such privilege find it easy to resent those who had the greater opportunity. Both sides of the equation must resist the temptation to sin, either through arrogance and assumption of right, or bitterness and resentment. Both are indicative of pride.

The upper class can feel that they have lost a great deal over the past two centuries, unfairly and through no fault of their own, and in many individual circumstances that is true. Well-meaning people who have worked for the good of others have seen their wealth and opportunities plummet compared to what they were. It is, however, hard for those struggling to put the heating on to feel sorry for them. After all, posh people still dominate the leadership positions of the country and have many of the best jobs; it is very likely that a posh accent will open doors to ministry training and positions, too. At the same time there is considerable prejudice against the upper class. 'Unconscious bias' training events will frequently accuse those who are white and posh (and, especially, male) of having inevitable attitudes of discrimination. They can be told that their mere existence causes offence to others. This attitude is sheer class prejudice, as much as snobbishness is. It is hard for posh people not to feel a pariah in these settings. Similar experiences can happen in Christian settings, where middle-class church groups would rather pretend, for the sake of political correctness, that posh people are just not there – or that they deserve, all the time, to be put down.

This is sad, when many posh Christians have taken on lives of sacrifice and service to the gospel. They are often in a position to accomplish a lot. It is worth remembering that the Evangelical Revival of the eighteenth century, which saw extensive evangelistic ministry to ordinary people across the country (and internationally), was greatly helped by upper-class people such as the Countess of Huntingdon (1707–1791); William Wilberforce (1759–1833), Charles Simeon (1759–1836) and J. C. Ryle (1816–1900) also spring to mind as extremely influential gospel workers.

Over the past century or so a new effort was put into reaching the ruling class with the gospel. This was part of a deliberate strategy to evangelise the nation and the world. It was thought that the characteristics of leadership described above were what was needed to take the gospel out to others. Leaders in mission were wanted, and so those who were already being trained to be leaders were evangelised. The strategy has merit, and had notable good results; although it has also had its failures. Secular leadership qualities are not always the same as the servant leadership shown by Christ.

Evangelism still goes on effectively through the camps for independent school students, and public school chaplaincies, which can be very effective. Such evangelistic efforts have spread into university ministry more generally. It is the reason why evangelical churches are dominated by the university educated and many evangelical networks are led by posh accents. It did not, however, spread much further. There was no trickle-down effect, as had been hoped. In that sense, the strategy failed. What is needed now is an equally determined push to reach the bulk of the population who are beyond these circles, and will probably always be.[2]

---

2 This chapter is notably lacking in footnotes. It is hard to find serious research on upper-class evangelicals; most of this information came from personal conversations and lived history. Published information is mostly in the form of informal blogs or sensationalized media reports.

Chapter 6

In defence of the middle class?

E ven the middle class tends to be very judgemental of the middle class. However, there is a reason why this class has expanded to include such a large percentage of the population. It is because it is actually what most people want; and in some ways, that is not a bad thing. A lot of biblical values do lead into a lifestyle that looks something like the middle class. Such values can, of course, be corrupted or used to serve selfish ends; but not everything about being middle class is bad. It is worth considering what we may want to preserve.

For instance, education *is* good. Christianity has always promoted literacy and learning; we worship a God who speaks and gives us his word, and who expects us to work to listen and understand. Christians have always built schools and preserved written sources. Education also helps people have more secure and interesting work lives. For all that the current university system is criticised and its failings acknowledged, it is still the case that having a degree means having a higher income. Gaining a degree, then, might not be an absolute value, but could still be considered something that is good to have. It is reasonable to want people to have the financial benefits of education (bringing warmth, health and freedom from the stress of poverty) as well as the intellectual and emotional benefits. It is good for people to have some choices and the ability to thrive and develop their gifts. The power that goes along with this is a healthy power that can be used for good. We do not want people to be ground down by their situation.[1]

There are good things about being middle-class; and becoming a Christian is at least part of what, historically and in the present, drives the creation of the middle class. Becoming Christian makes lives more ordered and moral. It teaches people to oppose illegal drug use and alcohol abuse, it sees priority given to looking after children and teaching them well, it values faithfulness and truthfulness and hard

---

1 And they are. The view that upper-middle class students tend to do better at school because they are more intelligent, and that this continues because people tend to marry within their own class, has been around for decades and refuses to die. However, research demonstrates that working-class background pulls students down despite cognitive ability. See Bastian A. Betthäuser, Mollie Bourne and Erzsébet Bukodi, 'Understanding the mobility chances of children from working-class backgrounds in Britain: How important are cognitive ability and locus of control?' *British Journal of Sociology* (2020), 1–17.

work. These things can all be practiced in any class situation, but it often leads to the kind of upwardly-mobile society that develops a middle class. It is not surprising that working class Christians often become more middle class, and their children even more so. And that's not entirely a bad thing. One Christian reflects:

> It's only since I came to faith in Jesus that I have started working full-time for the first time in my life, and now I take financial responsibility for my family in a legal way (Rob, early 40s).[2]

Academic studies have shown that faith has an objective effect on the ability to take on middle-class aspirations such as university education. For instance, research has shown that faith helps British Black African Caribbean men achieve academically, because it helps them to overcome lack of middle-class educational habitus.

> Middle-class players are more dominant within the field of education, as they enter the educational poker game in a more privileged capital position due to the habitus-formation process of their upbringing and family connections.[3]

2 Quoted in McConnell, *The Least the Last and the Lost*, 80. Mez McConnell is one of several working-class commentators on the church who became a Christian and became middle class, in the sense of becoming educated and owning a home. His ministry on the Nidrie scheme has seen people get work, retrain, and go to university (429).

3 Constantino Dumangane Jr, 'The significance of faith for Black

For a working-class person, who did not grow up with middle-class assumptions embedded into their family and schooling, the higher education system can be extremely daunting. If reading books is not normal and praiseworthy, it can be a hard habit – not to mention skill – to acquire. How to listen to a lecture, how to take notes, how to understand what is required from an essay question – these can be real barriers. University teachers and educational research certainly take more notice of such issues now than in the past, but there are still a host of cultural assumptions and difficulties that make university life objectively much harder for someone from a working-class background.

> [P]lacing a working-class habitus in a middle-class education system increases the likelihood of alienation and conflict for working-class students ... In some cases, BACM [British African Caribbean men] culture is removed from White middle-class behaviourally accepted norms within the education field, which can lead to isolation of these students within such educational fields. However, it is suggested that faith may be an influential poker chip that can assist BACM to reduce some of the imbalance they experience in the educational poker game field.[4]

---

men's educational aspirations', *British Educational Research Journal* 43.5 (2017): 875–903, 878.

4 Dumangane, 'The significance of faith', 879.

In other words, faith acts as a resource, or a kind of capital, that can help students with a working-class habitus 'to address challenges and manage and/or acclimate within these environments'.[5] This can happen in five ways:

> (1) Faith as a motivator and a form of protection from destructive behaviours.

> (2) Church and faith as a source of skill acquisition, application and support.

> (3) Faith participation and protective and aspirational influences.

> (4) Parents, faith and effects associated with prayer.

> (5) Faith's influence on civil society and community-focused goals.[6]

Going to church in itself can help with obtaining an educational habitus; the practice of sitting and listening to a sermon, being able to concentrate for that long and absorb a linear and (hopefully) logical flow of ideas is good training for

---

5 Dumangane, 'The significance of faith', 880.

6 Dumangane, 'The significance of faith', 887. Dumangane also mentions that 'Excessive drinking as a social event at university was another factor that four of the six participants' narratives discussed being able to avoid due to their faith involvement on campus' (889). However, I have found that in many contexts middle-class evangelical Christians drink quite a lot.

education. Such skills are transferable to other contexts. Other ways in which working-class students testify that church helped their education was that 'religious beliefs developed their character through discipline, respect and morality'. One student added that the church 'acted as a network of support for him after his father's death, which upholds previous research findings on the supportive benefits that faith may provide'.[7] Another learned:

> How to read something and get some meaning out of it. How to communicate that succinctly to somebody else in public. And what was effective. You know like the idea of giving a speech or talking in public about something.[8]

US research has found that young Black people from socio-economically deprived backgrounds who attended church services and youth groups were helped in their education. If we think in terms of social and cultural capital, church can give these kinds of capital even when a person's class background does not. This can help young people in behaviours and practices that are beneficial for educational

---

7 Dumangane, 'The significance of faith', 890. We should be encouraged that long sermons are a good thing; we can help attention spans increase, rather than reducing sermon length and depth to catch attention.

8 Dumangane, 'The significance of faith', 890. This, of course, only holds if people are given the chance – and encouragement – to take on leadership in church contexts.

settings.

Another quality that was seen to come from attending church was the ability to delay gratification. One student reports:

> I think because everybody (pause) everyone looked at things in a very short-term manner. They wanted everything instantly. This culture of instant gratification. Like quick money. You know get things quickly. They never thought long term. Most of the people around me ... always thought about the now rather than the future. And from that you've got a lot of people who ... were just working in order to just spend on material things like clothes, trainers. [But] ... when I started getting into my church I found youths who were very long-term thinkers ... and they knew what they wanted. And I wanted to be one of those people, you know. I wanted to know what I wanted.[9]

Do we want Christians to be middle class? Yes, in some ways, we do. There are good things about typical middle-class attributes such as the valuing of education, of hard work, of ordered lives, and of a certain quality of culture. Indeed, society in general appears to agree:

---

9 Dumangane, 'The significance of faith', 891. See also Cheron Byfield 'The impact of religion on the educational achievement of Black boys: A UK and USA study', *British Journal of Sociology of Education* 29.2 (2008): 189–199.

> It's not just the church but society [that] wants people to be middle class, often even working-class people, or they want what middle-class people have got ... media portrays the lower working class in such a way that it's so undesirable; who wants to become a chav?[10]

Yet is it really necessary to be middle-class to have these things? Changing class is costly, in energy, in personal dislocation, and in relationships. It is emotionally costly. What is more, while we want to promote the educational skills that help in understanding the Bible, there is no requirement that these be translated into secular education and social mobility. The status achieved in this way can be challenged by the gospel itself. There are alternative ways to think of what a successful life is. There are certainly Christian advantages in helping people to stay where they are. As one working-class Christian reports:

> I'm living here to serve Jesus, no one else is going to do it so we are going to do it, so we are going to stay here. And that's something I try to, so some of my sermons are just encouraging people to stay living on the estate and say let's glorify God in this place.[11]

There is a good deal to be said in developing a new, work-

10 McKenzie, 'The Person God Made Me to Be', 9.

11 McKenzie, 'The Person God Made Me to Be', 9.

ing-class way of being a genuine Bible-based Christian; in gaining a sense of status and worth from God's salvation rather than from societal ideas of upward mobility.[12] We want people to live godly and quiet lives (Titus 2:12; 1 Thessalonians 4:11), obeying God's commands (Matthew 28:20) and teaching each other the gospel (Colossians 3:16). But it is not necessary to adopt all the manners and habits of the middle class in order to do so. The trick is separating out what is middle-class and what is actually Christian.

Do we want working-class Christians to become middle class? In some ways, we do. In other ways, we do not. We should certainly not assume that the fact that the gospel and church-going can teach an ability to become middle class means that this is therefore the goal for all Christians. That is an assumption that, as we have seen, makes it harder for working-class people to become Christians. We don't want people to feel too uncomfortable at church, or in Christian groups, to walk in. That's as bad as the 1 Corinthians 14:23 problem, where Paul chastised the church for being so disorderly that outsiders coming in think the church members are out of their minds.

Is that what we do to non-middle-class people who

---

12 Of course, this would not really be new. Throughout history and all over the world, there have been working-class Christians. It is just something that the evangelical church has lost more recently.

come into our churches? It seems that, at least in some cases, we do.

> I had to go through a bloody culture war first, something that very few people back then understood, and nobody had warned me about. It turns out that there really is a great cost to following Jesus.[13]

We do not want people to have to go through an unnecessary culture war simply in order to be Christian. That is to tie millstones around convert's necks. People should not be made to feel unwelcome.

At the same time, there is a cost to following Jesus, and part of comfortable middle-class Christianity is to make that cost invisible for middle-class Christians. They were nice, polite people before; and they continue nice, polite people afterwards. Whatever class we are from, our churches probably could do more to make being Christian distinctive. Maybe it would be better for a lot of middle-class Christians if they did face a cost to becoming Christian. We certainly need to challenge the unconscious greed and selfish ambition that is so comfortably accepted in evangelical churches, and such a normal thing to teach children. It is good for there to be a cost to following Jesus; it forces Christians to be conscious about their priorities. It is a way to prove that faith is genuine, and

---

13 McConnell, *The Least, the Last and the Lost*, 15.

it is a way for Christians to be distinctive. Both would be very good for us, of any class.

Afterword: middle-class communication

The English middle class are often described, criticised, de-rided and caricatured as being unable to express what they really mean. I have heard this from commentators of all classes, including the middle classes themselves. Sometimes it's put positively; middle classes prioritise not hurting people's feelings, whereas the working classes prioritize honesty.

I'm not sure that's the right way to put it. Middle-class people can be honest and they do express what they mean. You just have to understand the language in which it is expressed.[14] And working-class people are concerned for feelings; they are often honest *in the interest of* people's feelings, so that people can feel they are not being lied to.

Middle-class people, for instance, will very openly let you know when you have outstayed your welcome. They will never do it, however, by saying 'it's time to go home now'. They will do it by other means, for instance, offering a second cup of tea. And this is very clearly understood, too, as I discovered when time after time my lunch guests would leave

---

14 I was greatly helped by linguist Deborah Tannen in this respect (see Deborah Tannen *That's Not What I Meant!: How Conversational Style Makes or Breaks Relationships* (New York: Ballantine Books, 1987), or the DVD of the same title). She explains that people of all cultures are quite capable of expressing exactly what they mean; but you need to understand the language styles of different cultures to be able to *hear* what they mean.

when I offered them a second cup of tea. I was usually dismayed; for me, it was a way of trying to extend their stay because I wanted them there. I just didn't yet know the language. Once it was explained to me, I knew; and I eventually realised that the way to accomplish my goal, to express what I really meant (that they should stay longer), was by suggesting we go for an after-lunch ramble. That was usually very well-received, and would be followed by more tea.

It was a learning experience for me. I was not part of a class war, yet even so I found it embarrassing. When I listen to cross-class conversation between British people – or, even more enlightening, different British classes talking about each other – offense and frustration are more common.

Working-class people are different from the middle class. They will express what they mean in more direct sentences. This does not mean they are favouring honesty over feelings, or don't care about feelings. They just express their honest meaning differently; and they will care for people's feelings by addressing them directly. (In many ways, the upper-class do as well.)

The British classes are so different that we need to have a mindset of cross-cultural ministry, requiring learning a new language. This may help to overcome some of the mutual antagonism.

Chapter 7

Theological education

One of the ways in which working-class people are said to be excluded from evangelical ministry is the emphasis on theological training, and the need for formal (degree) qualifications in order to be a minister. As Williams and Brown put it:

> [W]e need to address deep-seated levels of class bias that honour formal qualifications above all attributes and reconsider how we develop and train our leaders.[1]

Why do church leaders need to have a degree? The simple answer is: they don't. What they do need, however, is a knowledge of how to teach the Scriptures, which means a good knowledge of what the Scriptures say and how to read them. That is *enormously* enhanced by a raft of other skills, which at the moment are most commonly and efficiently taught through university-ratified tertiary education institutions. What are these other skills that so greatly help to teach the Bible well?

The first is knowing the original languages, something

---

1 Williams and Brown, *Invisible Divides*, 18.

I have often heard criticised by working-class Christians (and, to be fair, Christians of all other classes) as unnecessary, esoteric and specialist. That is not true. Knowing the biblical languages is enormously helpful in maintaining faithful and accurate preaching. Yes, they are hard to learn. It is a great shame that language teaching in general is not much more common in schools, which would make learning a new language as an adult much easier. We can only work with what we have; that does not change the fact that learning biblical languages should be seen as commonplace for Bible teachers.

Bible teachers also need a grasp of what the Bible teaches overall on particular topics about God, humans, and the world. That is, they need a good knowledge of doctrine, and they need a good knowledge of how our understanding of these topics develops throughout the Bible. They need both systematic and biblical theology. Otherwise they will not be teaching particular passages in the context of the whole Bible, and so will not be teaching Scripture accurately.

It is greatly helpful, in coming to understand the Bible and its doctrine, to know at least some church history – to learn from other Christians throughout the ages who have studied Scripture themselves and who have had to fight battles to keep to its truth. Bible teachers also have to know how to teach practically; how to do their exegesis of a particular passage, how to construct a sermon, effective ways of teaching, effective ways of applying to people. Pastors teach *people*. Pastors have to know their congregations to preach to them (also an argument against mega-churches, but that's a different issue).

That is why training pastors for word ministry includes these things. But there are, in our current way of running churches, other things that a pastor has to do. Knowing people and dealing with personal issues is greatly helped by some knowledge of counselling and psychology; running a team of staff or volunteers is helped by having knowledge of management; there are also planning and organisational skills, running children's work and youth groups, the practicalities and legalities of weddings and funerals and church buildings, dealing with public and cultural issues, and knowing apologetics.

There is a lot that goes into training a minister with enough to keep him or her going throughout a lifetime of ministry (and it should also include ongoing training). This is why training for ministry needs to be taken seriously; it will take dedicated time, and it needs churches to provide adequate funding.

But does it need a degree? No, not necessarily. The university system, however, is already there, set up to provide structure and accountability in educating people. It has been very useful for theological colleges to ally themselves with them.

Yet it doesn't have to be that way. The university way of teaching has major drawbacks, something that many university teachers themselves have tried to combat. Strategies such as flipping the classroom,[2] changing assessment structures, and challenging the unwritten curriculum, are efforts to overcome the bias towards a particular kind of learning that assumes a particular kind of background. These efforts often struggle in the current system which is so top-heavy and bureaucratic.

The modern Western university system also has all the drawbacks of modern secularism, which will mount an increasingly hostile opposition to traditional Bible training. This is certainly something that churches will need to take into account as they consider the future of theological education. That education, however, still has to happen. Theological education is still necessary.

The teaching of all the subjects mentioned above could certainly be done, and may well be done better, in less formal settings; apprenticeship-type models, in-church training and so on. Jesus taught his disciples without any university being

---

2 'Flipping the classroom' describes a teaching strategy in which valuable face-to-face time is not spent in imparting information (which can be done through a recorded lecture, or readings, which students take in at their own pace beforehand). Class time is instead spent in discussion, or problem-solving, or other types of active learning.

involved.

But it has to be done properly. Current alternatives for ministry training don't always work. 'On the job' training is very often severely lacking in content; students just don't get the 'information' part of formation if they are not having hours in which they are taught it. Jesus taught informally, but he did teach, privately and publicly. The disciples lacked formal education, but probably had hours as boys hearing the Scriptures taught in the synagogue. Paul certainly had a great deal of formal learning.

Part of our problem, of course, is that churches themselves are not teaching congregations enough. There's a lot more that children could learn (whatever class they come from) if we were prepared to make the effort. Where are the Sunday Schools of yesteryear? My Presbyterian friends remember not having just memory verses, but memory chapters, not to mention their Westminster catechising; an excellent foundation for understanding biblical doctrine.[3]

So yes, absolutely, recruit working class ministers. And let us be adventurous in setting up structures that allow them

---

3 Incidentally, Anglicans also have (much under-utilised) catechisms. See Ash Carter, Ros Clarke, and Lee Gatiss, *Walk This Way: Guided Reflections on Christian Faith, Life, and Prayer for Individuals and Groups* (London: Church Society and Lost Coin Books, 2020) and Martin Davie, *Instruction in the Way of the Lord: A Guide to the Catechism in the Book of Common Prayer* (London: Latimer, 2014).

to train. That includes funding them so that they don't have to keep working full-time while they do it. Theological training is demanding enough without requiring money-earning work on top of it. Practical work in a church can certainly be part of theological training, but it is only *training* if it is accompanied by proper supervision, preparation, debriefing and discussion.

It is worth adding to this discussion that we must train women as well as men. We need women to be teaching women in churches; this means they need theological training, as men do. Yet it is often much harder for women to access training financially, not to mention the encouragement and moral support to do it. Theologically trained women are especially necessary if we are to be reaching the working classes. Sharon Dickens writes that UK women 'are more likely to be living in deprived areas and struggling with poverty than men'; she adds that we must be aware of '... the need for more and more women to be theologically trained to reach the least, the last and the lost among the female population living in our council estates and housing schemes'.[4] These women need evangelists and Bible teachers, not just social workers.

Is the answer in-house church-based training? Possibly. Nonetheless, there are considerable advantages to centralised training, financially as well as in terms of quality. A

4 Sharon Dickens, in McConnell, *The Least, the Last and the Lost*, 89.

few highly specialised teachers can teach a lot of students at once if they all come to the same centre. The students then also get the benefit of a range of different specialities, *precisely because* we are not training the students to be specialists but generalists. Hands-on training in ministry is also a necessary part of the system; that is why we have apprenticeships beforehand and curacies afterwards. There are other ways of organizing theological training, but they need to work.

Formal, degree-based training for ministry can be difficult for working-class people, because they frequently have not had the educational preparation for it that middle-class people have. Joanne McKenzie, in her interviews with evangelical ministers, reports that working-class students 'often ... talked of the great emotional and spiritual benefits of the course.' Middle-class students did as well, 'But middle-class students did not express any of the discomfort.' One working-class student described his experience of theological training this way:

> I was accepted [for ministry training] and I went and, do you know what, it was the best thing that I have ever done; it's been the most challenging, spiritually and personally and emotionally. I went there and I was like, no one intentionally set out to make me feel like I didn't fit in, that's the part of the council estate chip on my shoulder, made me feel like as soon as I turned up and heard people from Lancashire sounding

like they were from, I don't know, but they just sounded, they weren't Lancashire ... They were either doctors, I think someone on that course would be poorly qualified if they were a teacher (*laughs*); do you know what I mean? So like Oxbridge educated, some of the theological terms that they were using I couldn't even spell, I couldn't even pronounce never mind spell them ...

The opportunities that are out there for training really require confidence. I mean, when I applied ... to do a theology degree it was so intimidating and I so nearly gave up a number of times. And part of me was thinking, 'Michael, who do you think that you are trying to get a theology degree, don't you know you're from an estate, you shouldn't be getting a theology degree'.[5]

What can we do to help those without a middle-class background to cope more easily with theological training? Churches could certainly do more to prepare students; as we saw in a previous chapter, churches that make an effort to train their teenagers for ministry also help them obtain the skills necessary for tertiary education.[6] Churches could also

5 McKenzie, 'The Person God Made Me to Be', 6.

6 After World War I, the large number of working-class men coming forward for ordination forced the Church of England to rethink preparation for ministry; in particular, how to help students obtain the level of education necessary to start theological training. One result was the establishment of the Knutsford Test

promote the necessity of theological training by encouraging it, supporting students financially, and supporting charities that promote theological education – this all helps overcome the culture shock that theological training can be.

Or maybe the answer is to invent a whole new way of doing rigorous theological training. If we do, working-class ministers must have a voice in its design. We need practical, efficient and cost-effective ways of providing the kind of comprehensive theological training that will support a minister through years of the hard work of church ministry.

It is worth it. Now, more than ever, we want thoroughly trained ministers of the gospel, for the sake of reaching all classes. It is possible; let us do it.

School, a fully funded full-time residential course, which ordination candidates attended for six to nine months before going onto university or a theological college. This provided the chance not only to bring candidates up to an academic standard where they might enter university, but also allowed teachers to be able to assess men for their personal suitability for ministry. See Robert Reiss, *The Testing of Vocation: 100 years of Ministry Selection in the Church of England* (London: Church House Publishing, 2013), 88–92.

Chapter 8

Mercy ministries: reaching the poor through social action

Throughout the Bible, God shows his heart for the poor and vulnerable, and as Christians we are to share his values. It is good to care for the poor. Should this be the powerhouse of our work to reach people?

Poverty and class are not the same issue, but they are closely related. In general, middle-class people are wealthier than working-class people; and there are definitely people in severe deprivation in the schemes, estates or on the streets of Britain. One of the signifiers of middle classness is the university degree, and degree still increases average earning, even with student loans to pay off.

There are plenty of poor in Britain.

14% of people in the UK were in absolute low income before housing costs in 2022/23, and 18% were in absolute low income (absolute poverty) after housing costs.[1]

Poverty is complicated or made worse by immigration problems, and immigrants are amongst the poorest in the country. Mental ill-health also contributes to the problems. Poverty itself can bring about mental ill-health; not having enough causes great anxiety; and the cycles of powerlessness and deprivation are very depressing. Escape via substance abuse is also common. Domestic violence is also a serious issue and is not getting any better. None of these problems is unique to the poor, but they are all worse amongst the poor, and they are all made worse by being poor.

This book is not about helping the poor *per se*, although that is obviously a good thing for Christians to do (Galatians 2:10; James 1:27).[2] But even more than that, we are interested in bringing the good news of Jesus to the poor. That is the greatest gift we can give any person, for it is of eternal value, not just for this life. It is also true that coming to know Christ, and the present-life benefits that brings, can also help people materially. We want to help people in both

1 House of Commons Library, 'Poverty in the UK: Statistics' (8 April 2024): 7, https://commonslibrary.parliament.uk/research-briefings/sn07096/.

2 A major tactic in helping the poor is preaching contentment, and against greed, to everyone. Poverty is greatly exacerbated by the accumulation of resources by the rich. Claudio Oliver, 'Fight Wealth Not Poverty', *Plough* (22 April 2024).

ways; and if we are to reach people, we need to understand how they live and go to where they are, emotionally as well as physically.

It is hard to escape poverty, and we want to help people do that. Yet what is the best way to do it? McConnell, surprisingly, says to stop the mercy ministries. Churches should stop their social justice programmes; food banks, warm banks and so on. Why? Because, essentially, they are often carried out in a degrading way. 'People can tell when we are happy to share the church's food with them, but wouldn't share our own.'[3] It is very easy for people to become projects, rather than people. Churches are willing to feed them, counsel them or otherwise aid them, but not befriend them. Not really. As McConnell says:

> [W]ould we sit down for a meal with those we are serving and supporting outside the confines of a church-based project? Or are projects a helpful way to do good to people 'not like us' while keeping them held firmly at arm's length?'[4]

The problem with charity projects, or social action, are their inherent judgementalism.

> Most project leaders and volunteers have a desperate desire to give dignity to everyone they help. However, any one of us can slip into a 'sav-

---

3 McConnell, *The Least, the Last and the Lost*, 68.

4 McConnell, *The Least, the Last and the Lost*, 69.

iour complex' that gives us an air of superiority – this is something we all need to watch in our own hearts. Also, no matter how much we try to run our projects in a way that honours people, there is something inherently undignified about turning up at an unfamiliar location where everyone knows you are in need.[5]

Such things can cause resentment, not gratitude. 'People can feel patronized and belittled by acts of charity if they perceive an attitude of superiority among those who are supporting them.'[6]

Mercy ministries, many commentators agree, are not the way to win the poor. Food banks and soup kitchens may be needed; so may be debt counselling and warm spaces. But needed isn't the same as wanted or appreciated; how would you feel if you had to accept charity for your food and shelter? It is embarrassing, and does not make people feel grateful.[7]

It may be good to help with such practical things, and if in your area there is real need, that may be a loving thing to do. However, find out just what is needed before thinking that is a useful way to direct church resources. Talk to peo-

5 Williams and Brown, *Invisible Divides*, 27.

6 Williams and Brown, *Invisible Divides*, 28.

7 I would recommend that everyone read George Orwell's *Down and Out in Paris and London* (London: Penguin Modern Classics, 1966), especially the account of being poor in London, for graphic and moving descriptions of how much those who need help can deeply resent the ways in which it is offered.

ple and ask them what would help most. It may be that what is really useful is to help people to access government aid, which for all its faults, is considerable. Find out if there are other social action projects already running, and get involved in them rather than duplicating efforts with something new. Better still, use your participation in an existing programme to build relationships. Befriend people. Talk to them. Relate to them as people. Or just do that, without the social action. Several times while talking to people about these chapters, I have heard the comment that social action projects are middle-class ideas to sooth middle-class consciences, not what the local poor would like to see set up.

At the very least, realise that poverty is not just about money. After all, as said above, there is a lot of help for the poor. The NHS is actually, in world terms, an astonishingly good system. British social services offer a great deal of aid, once the bureaucracy can be negotiated. But that's not all that poverty is about. Poverty is complicated. You may be living on an urban council estate, with enough income from benefits to have food and even heating, because your flat is fairly small. But you may be kept awake all night with sounds of violence outside. You may be afraid to go out and so spend most of your time inside. There may be too many of you inside so you never experience privacy or peace. Someone at home may be abusive so that you deliberately leave and become homeless rather than stay there. Or you may be technically safe there, but it is dreary and always unpleasant and you have no idea how to get out, how to become better educated or get a good job or live anywhere better. Poverty is debilitiating.

Do hospitality, not just food banks

> I've found that, so often, churches don't seriously consider the working-class communities on their doorstep unless it is in connection with social action.[8]

Too often, our projects involve doing things for or to people, not with them. To engage with people, involve them in church life and our own lives, is harder; but that is to treat people as people.

Meeting people does not have to happen inside your home, if others are not comfortable there. Social meeting can happen in other places; hospitality outside the home. I noticed that a local pub was full on Christmas Eve and Christmas Day; that is where people were meeting and gathering, sharing their lives and celebrations. I can also remember a time when I had to visit a church on a Sunday morning to hear a student give a talk. I had arrived too early, and the only place open where I could get a coffee was the local pub. On that early hour on a Sunday morning the pub was full of men, sitting alone. Where were the men from church, to meet

8 Williams and Brown, *Invisible Divides*, 13.

them and get to know them? It probably wouldn't occur to most Christian men to visit the pub on a Sunday morning; but what an opportunity!

We have discussed in an earlier chapter the problems of hospitality via the middle-class dinner party. Many writers on working-class culture agree that a drop-in culture is more common; something that middle class people struggle with. However, if we give up some of our ideas of what 'entertaining' requires, it could be easier. Let people drop in, and just be there. Let our houses be more porous.

Of course, if people are to drop in, they have to be within easy distance – we have to be living nearby. That raises another issue, of where we live. Most middle-class evangelicals live in comfortable middle-class enclaves. This will be discussed in our next chapter, and may be the evangelical church's greatest challenge in reaching the working classes.

Chapter 9

How to reach the working class

There seem to be two main areas that need to be tackled by evangelical churches if they are truly going to offer a ministry to working class people on any scale. They involve addressing the problems in existing churches, and planting new churches.

Changing the existing church culture

Many of the comments from working-class people point out the basic problem in church culture –that middle-class values have taken over, and are conflated with Christian values. This makes Christian churches hard to navigate or even to enter, for working-class people. If that is the case, then we need to change church cultures to make them more genuinely welcoming. This means that we stop conflating Christian morality with middle classness. In turn, that means a serious push to teach biblical Christian ethics. This could involve a few things:

Challenging middle-class problems

There are several ways in which it appears that many middle-class churches fail to preach true biblical ethics. How much do we challenge middle-class Christians about greed, which the Bible overtly identifies as idolatry? What about the assumption that life must involve growing in wealth? How much teaching is there on giving sacrificially? On challenging the idol of education and 'good' schools for children? What counts as a good school?

Why is it that Christians ever think it is appropriate to have a career, rather than a job? How much do we teach that work is for the purpose of feeding one's family, and being generous – and not personal gain? How much is individualism overtly challenged in teaching and example? As one researcher points out, after interviewing working-class Christians:

> Interviewees identified aspects of middle-class culture such as materialism, an excessive focus on career and individualism as negative and aspects of working-class culture such as a sense of community and commitment to care for the elderly as positive.[1]

In general, it seems that the poorer people are, the more they are prepared to give. The middle class does not do well in this regard. C. S. Lewis said of Christian giving that the only safe

1 McKenzie, 'A Different Class?', 179.

rule is to give more than we think we can. In fact, he went so far as to say that if we have the same standard of living as others in our income bracket, then we are not giving enough. We should actually feel deprived to some extent because of what we give away.[2]

Preparing working-class people for leadership

Church should be a place where people get the opportunity to use their gifts for the common good – the purpose for which such gifts are given. Those with gifts of leadership, or potentially with them, need chances to lead. They need to be able to learn and practice skills, and grow in confidence and capability. That does not always happen for working class people.[3] It may require conscious effort on the part of existing leadership. In many cases, even those working-class people who may be gifted do not necessarily want to accept lay leadership responsibility, having no background that normalises or prepares them for leadership; while middle-class people are all too eager to assume it. This may mean mean pushing people forward who resist, and holding others back who are offended that they are not being given opportunities. In both cases, teaching true Christian values must be a priority.

---

2 C. S. Lewis, *Mere Christianity* (William Collins: 2016, first published 1942), 86.

3 McKenzie, 'A Different Class?', 183.

Teach real change of identity

All Christians are a new creation in Christ. If these 'new creations' look exactly like the world around us, then just how Christian are we being? Every Christian must be challenged to put off the old, to question old ways of behaving, old ways of thinking, old identities. Questioning of assumptions in the face of biblical teaching should be normal. Insofar as working-class people might have to change to fit in with Christian culture, middle-class people should have to change just as much. There is a right challenging of all cultures and identities when coming to Christ.

Overall, our churches need to be places where Christ's values are reflected, whatever your group. Everyone needs to be considering others better than ourselves (Philippians 2:3); more needing of our attention, more worthy of our time. That requires learning a certain astuteness and sensitivity to other people and how they might be perceiving this conversation, this church, this offer of hospitality or whatever it is. It's for all Christians to learn, for this is loving our neighbour as ourselves.

Talking to people

One specific piece of advice from Williams and Brown is that we should not always start conversations by asking people questions about themselves. I must admit, this is the opposite of what I have been taught. I was never a natural conversation-maker; I learned how to make conversation by observation and asking good conversation-makers what they do. I have been taught that in Britain the way to show interest in people is to ask questions about the person. The advice I have received is that to do so is not just polite, but that it makes the person feel at ease and welcomed. So I have persevered in doing it, even though I often feel very intrusive, and I don't always like it when people do it to me.

Yet Williams and Brown suggest that this is a particularly middle-class phenomenon. Their example is Glenn, from a 'chaotic working-class background'; 'in his previous experience, it was the police and those in authority who asked those intrusive questions, and people like Glenn wouldn't usually trust those in authority'.[4] They suggest starting conversations with something more neutral, such as the weather. I remember a wise pastor saying that to talk to anyone, you need to learn to talk about common interests: sport, gardening, and pets.

Conversations, and indeed preaching, could be consciously broader in its scope and applications. If you are telling a salutary story about something your child said, is it necessary to add that this conversation took place while you were driving your child to school? Some people do not have cars.

---

4 Williams and Brown, *Invisible Divides*, 58.

Is it necessary to include a sermon illustration about your overseas holiday? Some families do not have overseas holidays. Or holidays at all.

These are all ways in which to make our existing churches not just more open to working-class people, but (I would suggest) more Christian. Yet if we are serious about mission outside the middle class, a further step needs to be taken.

Put resources and people into reaching the working class

Ministry to the public-school educated became fruitful because decades of work was poured into evangelising these students – through the Iwerne 'Bash' camps; university ministry; city workers ministries and so on. Ministry to the urban middle classes is thriving because so many churches cater for them. All of these need more work and more evangelising; there are still many middle-class people who have not been reached. But if we are to reach the working classes, at least as much effort needs to be made for them.

The evangelical church was not always middle class. Bebbington reports that early evangelicalism (from the 1730s) was not middle-class. That does not mean it had mass support from the working classes (it is easy to romanticise the early evangelical movement); but it did include many skilled workers (59 percent of Evangelical Nonconformists were classified as skilled artisans, as opposed to 23 percent of the population of Britain).[5] This demographic changed, as mentioned earlier, because twentieth-century evangelicals concentrated on the public schools, universities and professions.

That effort reaped its reward, and it is good that so many middle- and upper-class people were converted. It was hoped that converting the 'leaders' of society would lead to conversions throughout society; but this 'trickle-down' theory of mission has not worked. This is not to say that converting potential leaders is a bad thing; we should, by all means, continue to try to. But it won't convert the country.

What could be the result if we made a similar effort, over generations, in working-class areas? What if evangelicals took the conscious decision to move house and plant churches, where the unreached people are? If they moved to council estates or schemes, to awkward rural areas (not just the pretty villages), lived there and got to know the people?[6]

It would probably not be easy. Moving to a council estate might make it harder to keep the children's well-ordered routines going. There may be late-night interruptions and raucous people around. It also might be a place where there

5 David Bebbington, 'God made them high or lowly: evangelicals and class', *Third Way* (April 1987): 10–14, 11.

6 Philip North, GS 2122 Estates Evangelism Task Group: Paper for the General Synod (2019), https://www.churchofengland.org/about/general-synod/agendas-papers/general-synod-february-2019#na.

is warmth of community and a real chance to share in people's lives. We need to live with people in order to be allowed to preach to them.[7]

It may mean a different kind of evangelism

To reach the working classes, have evangelistic events that serve pie and peas (or whatever it is people like – find out), not wine and cheese. Have them in the pub, not the church hall decorated with bunting. Have them around bingo, not art events. Find what will genuinely interest people – which means getting to know people. Don't charge admission if you're trying to attract poorer people. We need to find out what kind of evangelistic resources will catch people's interests, and through what media. We need to find out what time of day is best for invitations, or even if invitations to events are the way forward at all. It means talking to working class people, to the working-class Christians who are already converted and know their culture, to the small number of pastors who are already doing the work, and to the non-Christians who may have never even considered church. Why not?

Also, 'Don't farm out evangelism among the poor in your community to para-church organisations' says Mez McConnell.[8] It doesn't establish churches, and that is what is

---

7 See Andy Prime's excellent chapter in McConnell, *The Least, the Last and the Lost*.

8 McConnell, *The Least, the Last and the Lost*, 31.

really needed. 'Local children need a healthy local church in their communities far more than they need our yearly holiday Bible clubs or weekly drop-ins'.[9] So, we need to look at how to do that.

It may mean a different kind of church

'Churches should be vibrant communities of Christians who are meaningfully involved in each other's lives'.[10] Of course, some of them are; but we all need to be aware of the human tendency to be tribal, and work against this tendency. A great deal of the New Testament, in fact, is about just that. Williams and Brown ask a useful diagnostic question: do the people you are trying to reach consider you as 'us' or 'them'?

Knowing what kind of church to create, with what kind of teaching and ministry, may mean going back to Scripture with the aim of finding out just what it says to the questions that middle-class people do not normally ask. Scripture does have the answers, for all sorts of lives. As one working-class Christian discovered:

> Michael recalled the surprise he had initially felt when he found answers in the Bible to help him care pastorally for people in relation to the everyday issues they face on the estate. He had not heard such issues spoken about in other churches or within the wider evangelical movement:

9 McConnell, *The Least, the Last and the Lost*, 31.
10 Williams and Brown, *Invisible Divides*, 80.

Oh the Bible does talk about this! It was then that I kind of was like, hang on a minute there is a Christianity for council estates but it's not in the middle-class churches, they don't know ... the Bible is so relevant to my culture and all this stuff has been hidden from me and that was then what really got me thinking that the Bible is relevant for council estate culture. The middle-class churches I've been in, I don't think they ever think through these issues. It doesn't seem relevant to them but I want to mine the Bible and find all this stuff that speaks to my culture.[11]

The Bible answers all those questions that current church culture is ignoring. It may take being confronted with the seemingly impossible problems that drives us to look for them.

It will mean putting money and time into mission

If we want to reach the working classes – the council estates, the rural poor, deprived areas or simply the people in cities and towns who do not feel middle-class – we need to devote resources to those ministries. Plant churches, set up courses, run missions. If there are not enough working-class pastors to start with – and it seems that there are not – then we need to train up more. The first generations may have to suffer middle-class educational techniques because we can't get our heads around how to do it properly any other way. But then

---

11 McKenzie, 'The Person God Made Me to Be', 9.

they can work out how to do it better to train up more and more. It will take vision and determination to do it.

Involve working class people

'It is frustrating for those of us who have grown up in poverty on council estates to be secondary to the conversation on reaching our own communities', says McConnell.[12] So let us go and talk to some working-class Christians.[13] Be with them, and let them take the lead. It may take work to do so, especially if they have been brought up to believe they can never be leaders, especially leaders of working-class people. It will be frustrating because they will make mistakes, and they will do things less well than you can do them, or do them the wrong way (or what you think is the wrong way). It will require middle-class people learning, instead of assuming they know the answers.

Conclusion

Evangelical churches in Britain are not serving the working classes. There is no secret about that, and no lack of analysis to see that it's needed: in that sense, this book is not really necessary (or at least, it is nothing new). We need to get on

---

12 McConnell, *The Least, the Last and the Lost*, 259.
13 I have certainly been very enlightened and helpfully educated by the working-class pastors and church members who have talked to me during the course of this research.

and do it. Let us learn, and try. It will require sacrificial missionaries. It will require being uncomfortable. It may mean talking to people you wouldn't naturally spend time with, at times of day you don't want to be sociable, in places you don't want to be, wearing clothes you don't like and with food and drink you don't enjoy. Cross-cultural mission can be like that.

Not everyone will do this. But for those who can, the mission field is there, waiting.

Appendix: Some statistics

60 percent of people in Britain consider themselves working class because they believe their family background determines class rather than occupation or whether they went to university. 47 percent of those in managerial or professional jobs consider themselves working class. The proportion who consider themselves working class has not changed since 1983.[1]

21.3 percent of British people are in skilled manual occupations, and 22.6 percent in semi-skilled and unskilled manual occupations.[2]

59.1 percent of British households had all household members aged 16 years and over in employment during April to June 2023. 13.7 percent of households had no member of the

---

1 University of Oxford (30 June 2016), https://www.ox.ac.uk/news/2016-06-30-most-people-britain-today-regard-themselves-working-class.

2 Office for National Statistics (17 August 2023), https://www.ons.gov.uk/employmentandlabourmarket/peopleinwork/employmentandemployeetypes/bulletins/approximatedsocialgradeenglandandwales/census2021.

household in employment.[3]

In 2021, 1.1 million children (8.9 percent) lived in long-term workless households, up 1.0 percentage points on the previous year.[4]

77 percent of those in Britain say that class affects opportunities in Britain 'a great deal' or 'quite a lot'. 40 percent of those who identify as working class say movement between classes is very difficult, compared to only 27 percent of those who identify as middle class.[5]

Middle-class people are nearly 80 percent more likely to end up in professional jobs than those from a working-class background.[6]

0.9 percent of people in the most deprived parishes attend

3 Office for National Statistics (30 August 2023), https://www.ons.gov.uk/employmentandlabourmarket/peopleinwork/employmentandemployeetypes/bulletins/workingandworklesshouseholds/apriltojune2023.

4 Office for National Statistics (26 October 2022), https://www.ons.gov.uk/employmentandlabourmarket/peoplenotinwork/unemployment/bulletins/childrenlivinginlongtermworklesshouseholdsintheuk/2021.

5 National Centre for Social Research, 'British Social Attitudes 40' (2023), https://natcen.ac.uk/sites/default/files/2023-09/BSA%2040%20Social%20class.pdf.

6 Social Mobility Commission (30 April 2019) https://www.gov.uk/government/news/class-privilege-remains-entrenched-as-social-mobility-stagnates.

church, compared with 2.4 per cent in the least deprived, and 0.8 per cent on housing estates.[7]

7 Madeleine Davies, 'Is the C of E still a class-riddled act?', *Church Times* (25 June 2021), https://www.churchtimes.co.uk/articles/2021/25-june/features/features/is-the-c-of-e-still-a-class-riddled-act.

References

Ackers, Peter. 'Protestant Sectarianism in Twentieth-Century British Labour History: From Free and Labour Churches to Pentecostalism and the Churches of Christ'. *International Review of Social History*, 64 (2019): 129–142.

Bebbington, David. 'God made them high or lowly: evangelicals and class'. *Third Way* (April 1987): 10–14.

Betthäuser, Bastian A., Mollie Bourne, and Erzsébet Bukodi. 'Understanding the mobility chances of children from working-class backgrounds in Britain: How important are cognitive ability and locus of control?' *The British Journal of Sociology* 71.2 (2020): 349–365. https://doi.org/10.1111/1468-4446.12732

Bordieu, Pierre. *Outline of a Theory of Practice*. Cambridge: Cambridge University Press, 1977.

Braber, N., Ching, J., Jarman, J., Stevens, O., Robson, J., & Pautz, N. 'Is he a barrister or not?': A study on perceived and actual accentism at the Bar of England and Wales. *International Journal of Speech, Language and the Law* (2024). https://doi.org/10.1558/ijsll.25886.

Carter, Ash, Ros Clarke, and Lee Gatiss. *Walk This Way: Guided Reflections on Christian Faith, Life, and Prayer for Individuals and Groups*. London: Church Society and Lost Coin Books, 2020.

Davie, Martin. *Instruction in the Way of the Lord: A Guide to the Catechism in the Book of Common Prayer*. London: Latimer, 2014.

Davies, Madeleine. 'New selection framework seeks "unseen-called"'. *Church Times* (25 June 2021). https://www.churchtimes.co.uk/articles/2021/25-june/news/uk/new-selection-framework-seeks-unseen-called.

— 'Is the C of E still a class-riddled act?'. *Church Times* (25 June 2021). https://www.churchtimes.co.uk/articles/2021/25-june/features/features/is-the-c-of-e-still-a-class-riddled-act.

Dumangane Jr, Constantino. 'The significance of faith for Black men's educational aspirations'. *British Educational Research Journal* 43.5 (2017): 875–903.

Goodhart, David. *The Road to Somewhere: The New Tribes Shaping British Politics*. London: Penguin, 2017.

Hall, Sarah Marie. '"You're not from 'round 'ere, are you?" Class, accent and dialect as opportunity and obstacle in research encounters'. Pages 41–58 in *Engaging with Policy, Practice and Publics: Intersectionality and Impacts*. Edited by Sarah Marie Hall and Ralistsa Hiteva. Bristol and Chicago: Policy Press, 2020.

'"Let Justice Roll Down Like Waters": Exploring the Wellbeing of Working-Class Clergy in the Church of England: A Rally Cry for Change' (October 2023). https://www.churchofengland.org/sites/default/files/2023-10/focussed-study-4-working-class-clergy-wellbeing.pdf.

Levon, Erez, Devyani Sharma and Christian Ilbury. 'Speaking up: accents and social mobility'. The Sutton Trust, November 2022.

Lewis, C. S. *Mere Christianity*. William Collins: 2016, first published 1942.

McKenzie, Joanne. 'A Different Class? Anglican Evangelical Leaders' Perspectives on Social Class'. Pages 170–189 in Abby Day (ed.), *Contemporary Issues in the Worldwide Anglican Communion: Powers and Pieties*. Farnham: Ashgate, 2016.

— '"The Person God Made Me to Be": Navigating Working-Class and Christian Identities in English Evangelical Christianity'. *Sociological Research Online* 22.1 (2017): 213–225.

McKinnon, Andrew. 'Religion and Social Class: Theory and Method After Bourdieu'. *Sociological Research Online* 22.1 (2017): 161–173.

North, Philip. 'GS 2122 Estates Evangelism Task Group: Paper for the General Synod (2019)'. https://www.churchofengland.org/about/general-synod/agendas-papers/general-synod-february-2019#na.

Office for National Statistics, 'National Statistics Socio-economic Classification (NS-SEC)' https://www.ons.gov.uk/methodology/classificationsandstandards/otherclassifications/thenationalstatisticssocioeconomicclassificationnssecrebasedonsoc2010.

Savage, Mike, Fiona Devine, Niall Cunningham, Mark Taylor, Yaojun Li, Johs. Hjellbrekke, Brigitte Le Roux, Sam Friedman and Andrew Miles. 'A New Model of Social Class? Findings from the BBC's Great British Class Survey Experiment'. *Sociology* 47.2 (2013): 219–250.

House of Commons Library. 'Poverty in the UK: Statistics' (8 April 2024). https://commonslibrary.parliament.uk/research-briefings/sn07096/.

National Centre for Social Research. 'British Social Attitudes 40. (2023). https://natcen.ac.uk/sites/default/files/2023-09/BSA%2040%20Social%20class.pdf Office for National Statistics (17 August 2023), https://www.ons.gov.uk/employmentandlabourmarket/peopleinwork/employmentandemployeetypes/bulletins/approximatedsocialgradeenglandandwales/census2021.)

— (30 August 2023), https://www.ons.gov.uk/employmentandlabourmarket/peopleinwork/employmentandemployeetypes/bulletins/workingandworklesshouseholds/apriltojune2023.

— (26 October 2022), https://www.ons.gov.uk/employmentandlabourmarket/peoplenotinwork/unemployment/bulletins/childrenlivinginlongtermworklesshouseholdsintheuk/2021

Oliver, Claudio. 'Fight Wealth Not Poverty'. *Plough* (22 April 2024).

Orwell, George. *Down and Out in Paris and London*. London: Penguin Modern Classics, 1966.

Reiss, Robert. *The Testing of Vocation: 100 years of Ministry Selection in the Church of England*. London: Church House Publishing, 2013.

Skeggs, B. *Formations of Class and Gender: Becoming Respectable.* London: Sage, 1997. Smith, Greg and Linda Woodhead. 'Religion and Brexit: populism and the Church of England'. *Religion, State and Society* 46.3 (2018): 206–223.

Social Mobility Commission. (30 April 2019). https://www.gov.uk/government/news/class-privilege-remains-entrenched-as-social-mobility-stagnates.

'Social Mobility Barometer – public attitudes to social mobility in the UK'. (11 March 2021). https://www.gov.uk/government/publications/social-mobility-barometer-2021/social-mobility-barometer-public-attitudes-to-social-mobility-in-the-uk.

Tannen, Deborah. *That's Not What I Meant!: How Conversational Style Makes or Breaks Relationships.* New York: Ballantine Books, 1987.

University of Oxford. (30 June 2016). https://www.ox.ac.uk/news/2016-06-30-most-people-britain-today-regard-themselves-working-class.

Watson, Bob and Niamh Underhill. 'Working and workless households in the UK: April to June 2023'. https://www.ons.gov.uk/employmentandlabourmarket/peopleinwork/employmentandemployeetypes/bulletins/workingandworklesshouseholds/apriltojune2023

Reforming Church

Reforming Church is a book about revitalising churches in the Church of England. Written with insight and a depth of experience, it gives the highs and lows of revitalisation ministry as well as sage advice about bringing a church ministry to life.

Raw, real, and honest – the realities and challenges, mistakes and breakthroughs, are all reflected on, with the understanding that ultimately, God is the revital-iser of his Church and he will use anyone who offers themselves to serve and join him in this beautiful purpose."

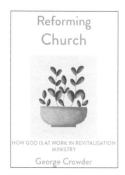

> *Rt Revd Dr Ric Thorpe (Bishop of Islington, The Gregory Centre for Church Multiplication)*

Please read and make widely known. If we ever need-ed revitalisation in the Church of England it is now.
> *Rt Rev Keith Sinclair (Former Bishop of Birkenhead)*

George's book is honest and realistic, wonderfully in-terweaving deep theology with lived experience, and is full of practical wisdom to inspire people to take up the challenge of revitalisation ministry.
> *Rt Rev Dr Rob Munro (Bishop of Ebbsfleet)*

£6 paperback or digital
UK orders direct from Church Society
www.churchsociety.org
admin@churchsociety.org | +44 1923 255410
Published by Church Society

Church Society

Gospel Flourishing
in a Time of Confusion

This book addresses key questions facing Anglican Evangelicals at this moment of confusion and uncertainty. Should we stay in the Church of England, and make use of the many gospel opportunities it affords? Or should we leave for pastures new, since things within the established church have become so difficult? What does it mean to be a "righteous remnant" in an apostate church, when everyone seems to be doing "what is right in their own eyes"? And are there lessons we can learn from how our ancestors handled these sorts of questions, not just in recent times but in the very earliest days of the church?

Five bishops, pastors, and theologians offer here a resource to help us think through the issues, that the gospel of Jesus might flourish and spread in our nation.

www.churchsociety.org * admin@churchsociety.org